"Come and See Kids"

Catholic Bible Study
for Children

The Life of Jesus

by

Laurie Watson Manhardt

Illustrated by

Aileen Co

Crafts by

Sandra Beyer

EMMAUS
ROAD
PUBLISHING

Steubenville, Ohio
A Division of Catholics United for the Faith

Emmaus Road Publishing
827 North Fourth Street
Steubenville, Ohio 43952

All rights reserved. Published 2005
Printed in the United States of America
First impression 2005

Library of Congress Control Number: 2004118250
ISBN 1931018286

Cover design and layout by
Jacinta Calcut/Image Graphics and Design
and Beth Hart

Cover artwork:
Christ Blessing the Children (Suffer Little Children), Antoine Ansiaux
Photo Credit: Réunion des Musées Nationaux/Art Resource, NY

Nihil obstat: Rev. Joseph N. Rosie, *Censor Librorum*
Imprimatur: ✠ John M. Smith
Bishop of Trenton
May 21, 2002

The *nihil obstat* and *imprimatur* are official declarations
that a book or pamphlet is free of doctrinal or moral error.
No implication is contained therein that those who have
granted the *nihil obstat* and *imprimatur* agree with
the contents, opinions, or statements expressed.

For additional information on the "Come and See"
Catholic Bible study series visit www. Catholicbiblestudy.net

"Come and See Kids"

Catholic Bible Study
for Children

Introduction	1
1) The Annunciation	3
2) The Visitation	9
3) The Nativity	14
4) The Shepherds and the Angels	19
5) The Magi	23
6) The Flight into Egypt	28
7) The Presentation	33
8) The Finding in the Temple	38
9) The Baptism of the Lord	43
10) Jesus' Temptation	49
11) Sermon on the Mount	56
12) The Lord's Prayer	61
13) Jesus Brings a Girl Back to Life	67
14) Jesus Feeds Five Thousand	73
15) Jesus Walks on Water	76
16) The Bread of Life	80
17) Jesus Works Miracles	83
18) Love One Another	89
19) Jesus Blesses Children	94
20) The Last Supper	100
21) The Crucifixion	106
22) The Resurrection	112
23) Jesus Lives!	118

Introduction

"The Life of Jesus" provides an opportunity for pre-school children to study the Bible while their mothers are doing Bible Study. The twofold benefit of blessing the children, while at the same time serving the mother with an opportunity to share her home study lesson in a small group without distraction, can be achieved when there are volunteers who feel called by God to serve as Children's Teachers.

Nurslings and small infants may stay in the small group with their mothers without distracting the other women in the group. Toddlers usually are best served by babysitters. Concern should be taken that a baby-sitter is minding an appropriate number of children to afford safety and a peaceful environment. If an adequate number of babysitters is not available, women should take turns volunteering to help the babysitter. Each woman is encouraged to help with the children, whether or not she has children of her own in the program. High school students and grandmothers also make wonderful babysitters and Children's Teachers.

Children's Teachers must have a love for God and a love for children. Formal education or teaching experience is not required.

Children from the ages of approximately two to five years of age could be served in a classroom setting, depending on their readiness and comfort in separating from mother. The Children's Teacher will be flexible in allowing mother to stay with the child for awhile and expect the child to cry a bit for the first few times when Mom leaves.

Initially, children could be allowed some playtime with toys, books or blocks. After playtime when all of the children have arrived, the Children's Teacher will make the Sign of the Cross, say a short prayer and read the Bible Story for the day to the children. The children can then color the accompanying picture and then work on crafts. Older children can work with pasting or cutting out figures. Children and teachers can "act out" the Bible Story, sing songs, march around the room and have fun. Try to sing and repeat the memory verse with the children.

A simple snack of animal crackers and water or goldfish crackers and juice could be provided. Mothers might take turns bringing snacks or contribute some money to purchase snacks. Remember to avoid nuts or chocolate, as some children may have allergies.

Small children memorize Bible verses well, often better than adults. Repetition helps the child remember the verse and the concept. Putting the verse to music can be a big help in learning Scripture. Try to fit the verse to a simple children's melody such as "Three Blind Mice" or "Frere Jacque." Singing makes memorizing easier for children. Memory verses can be repeated often during the day and again from week to week.

Each chapter in "The Life of Jesus" book includes a:
• **Bible Story** about "The Life of Jesus," followed by a
• **Picture** describing that story, which the child can color, and
• **Children's Craft**, outlined and explained in detail.

The Children's Teacher should read over the craft in advance, obtain necessary supplies and make a sample of the craft to show the children. After the teacher tells the Bible Story, the story may be acted out and then the children can work on the craft with some help.

Children can prepare a simple program of recitation, singing or drama to share with the adults at Christmastime or at the end of the class year. Everyone enjoys seeing the children perform, even if the Children's Teacher is doing most of the singing or reciting. It's just a delight to see the children God has given us, singing about Him.

A small group of children may be taught in one room. A larger number of children can be divided into age groups with small children in one room and older children in another. A cooperative program in which mothers take turns teaching the children might be considered as well.

Pray about what will work best in your given situation. Support a culture of life and try to welcome and embrace all of the mothers and children God sends your way. Please make sure that Children's Teachers also have an opportunity to share the home study questions in a small group later. The teacher should offer to stay after Bible Study to give a short repeat of the lecture to the Children's Teachers, or offer them an audio-tape of the lesson.

Essentially, pray for the children. Love the children. Be patient. Serve the mothers and children for the glory of God. Do the best you can with the resources you have. God doesn't expect perfection of us. He simply invites us to do our best for Him.

Pray, serve, and give God the glory!

The Annunciation
Luke 1:26-37

Memory Verse:
"Do not be afraid" (Luke 1:13).

The whole world was waiting for God to save people from their sin of disobeying God. Mary was waiting and praying too. While she was praying, the angel Gabriel appeared to her. Angel Gabriel told Mary that God had chosen her to be the Mother of God, to bring Jesus, the Messiah, into the world, to save us from our sin.

Mary was afraid. She had never seen an angel! Angels are spirits, messengers of God to guide and watch over us. You have a guardian angel who watches over you, too. Angel Gabriel told Mary: "Do not be afraid, Mary, for you have found favor with God. And behold, you will have a Son and you shall name him Jesus. He will be great, and will be called the Son of the most high . . . and of his Kingdom there will be no end" (Luke 1:31-33).

"Mary said to the angel, 'How can this be, since I have no husband?'

The angel said to her, 'The Holy Spirit will come upon you and . . . the child will be called holy, the Son of God'" (Luke 1:34-35).

Mary said, "I am the handmaid of the Lord, let it be done as you say" (Luke 1:38).

The angel also told Mary that her cousin, Elizabeth, a very old lady, would soon have a baby. For nothing is impossible with God (cf. Luke 1:37).

Mary carried Jesus under her heart. Mary is the Mother of God and the mother of all who believe in Jesus. When we pray, we ask Mary, our spiritual mother, to pray for us, sinners now and when we get ready to die. When we die, we want to die in God's grace so that we can see Jesus, face to face. Jesus can bring His friends into the throne room of God the Father in heaven.

We ask Jesus to forgive our sins and, when we die, to bring us into heaven, where we can live in the presence of God for all eternity. Eternity is forever, millions and billions of years! When we leave this world we hope to see all of our loved ones who have died before us.

Pray to your Guardian Angel to help you to love Jesus and be good and obedient. Pray to your Guardian Angel whenever you are afraid. Remember Angel Gabriel said, "Do not be afraid" (Luke 1:13).

Angel of God,

My guardian dear,

To whom God's love

commits me here,

Ever this day

be at my side,

To light, to guard,

to rule and guide.

Amen.

The Annunciation

Annunciation Craft

This craft will produce a decorative prayer book that when opened will present the "Hail Mary." (note: Later prayers will be combined with this prayer to create a wonderful Prayer Book for the child.)

Materials:

colorful foam paper, hole puncher, yarn, markers, stickers, glue, scissors, tape, "The Hail Mary" prayer printed on paper (4" x 6")

Preparation:

1. Fold and cut each piece of foam paper in half (short sides together). Each craft will use one piece of foam paper.

2. Punch holes around the rim of the foam paper.

3. Pre-print the "Hail Mary" prayer on paper. You can do this by hand or print two prayers per sheet of 8 1/2" x 11" paper on your computer using landscape mode. One prayer per child will be needed.

4. Cut 24" lengths of yarn (two per craft). Tie a knot at the end of each piece and place tape around the tip of the other side for ease of sewing.

5. Cut 10" pieces of yarn (one per craft) to be used as the book's binding.

Assembling:

1. Write "MY PRAYER BOOK" or personalize with the child's name "JOSHUA'S PRAYER BOOK" using markers in the center of one piece of pre-punched foam paper. Be sure to hold foam paper short side on top.

2. Decorate the cover of the prayer book with stickers or markers.

3. Thread the yarn in and out of the holes all the way around the foam paper. Tie a knot and cut off excess when you reach the first hole. Repeat for the other piece of foam paper.

4. Place the two foam pieces together (making the book) and punch two new holes in the center left side approximately 2-3 inches from each other.

5. Thread the small piece of yarn through the two holes, starting from the back. Tie a knot and then a bow in the front to bind the book together.

6. Open the book and write "The Hail Mary" on the inside cover.

7. Glue the pre-printed copy of the Hail Mary prayer on the facing page. The prayer book is now complete!

Other Ideas:

1. Use paper plates or poster paper instead of foam paper, if unavailable.

2. Decorate with holy cards, pictures from old Christmas cards, buttons, small pompoms, old puzzle pieces, etc. for the cover of the prayer book.

3. Use glitter/glue markers for writing "MY PRAYER BOOK" for a puffy or fancy look.

4. Add more pages with more prayers if time allows (The Lord's Prayer, Act of Contrition, Glory Be to the Father or Grace Before Meals).

5. Use ribbon instead of yarn for binding pages together.

The Visitation
Luke 1:39-45

Memory Verse:
"Hail Mary, full of grace, the Lord is with you."
(Luke 1:28)

When the angel Gabriel left, Mary went quickly to the house of her cousin, Elizabeth. Elizabeth and her husband, Zechariah, were very old people. They were sad because they didn't have any children or grandchildren.

An angel appeared to Zechariah to tell him that he and Elizabeth would have a baby, named John. Zechariah was afraid of the angel. He didn't believe the angel. He knew that he and Elizabeth were too old to have a baby. Zechariah forgot that "Nothing is impossible for God!" (Luke 1:37, NAB).

When Mary reached Elizabeth's house, Elizabeth's baby leaped in her womb and Elizabeth was filled with the Holy Spirit. Elizabeth said to Mary, "Blessed are you among women, and blessed is the fruit of your womb!" (Luke 1:42). Jesus is the fruit of Mary's womb. John the Baptist is Elizabeth's baby.

When we pray the "Hail Mary," we use the words that the Holy Spirit gave to Elizabeth along with the words the angel Gabriel said to Mary. How much of this prayer can you pray?

Where did the words of the "Hail Mary" prayer come from? The first words of the "Hail Mary" came from the Bible!

Hail Mary

Hail Mary, full of grace, the Lord is with you.
Blessed are you among women
and blessed is the fruit of your womb.
Holy Mary, Mother of God,
Pray for us sinners,
now and at the hour of our death.
Amen

Mary stayed with Elizabeth for three months and helped her prepared for the new baby. Elizabeth's new baby would be named John the Baptist. When John grew up and became a man, he would prepare the way for Jesus. What do you want to be when you grow up? Do you want to be helpful to other people like Mary, the Mother of Jesus was?

Visitation Craft

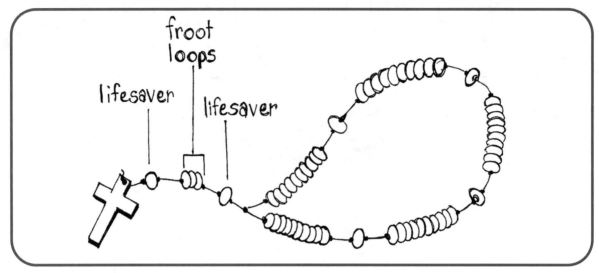

The children can make rosary beads using yarn, fruit-loops cereal and candy lifesavers. They can practice praying the Lord's Prayer and Hail Mary with this craft.

Materials:

yarn, foam paper, fruit-loops or cheerios breakfast cereal, candy life savers, hole puncher, scissors, tape

Preparation:

1. Trace and cut a small cross out of foam paper (2" x 3" in size). One cross per craft will be needed.

2. Punch a hole in the top of the cross.

3. Cut a 2" piece and a 10" piece of yarn (one for each craft).

4. Put tape around the ends of the yarn to allow for ease of threading the 'beads.'

5. Tie one end of the 10" piece of yarn to the cross using a knot.

Assembling:

1. Take the yarn attached to the cross and follow these instructions to create the opening prayer strand of the rosary beads.

    - Leave a small space (1") of yarn and tie a knot.
    - Put one life saver on the yarn and tie a knot.
    - Leave another small space (1") of yarn and tie a knot.
    - Put 3 fruit-loops on the yarn and tie a knot.
    - Leave a space and put another life saver on the yarn and knot.
    - Leave another small space of yarn; then tie another knot.

2. Then create the decades of the rosary (the necklace part.) Follow these instructions for each decade and repeat five times.

    - Leave a small space (1") of yarn and tie a knot.
    - Put 10 fruit-loops or cheerios on the yarn and tie a knot.
    - Leave another small 1" space of yarn and tie a knot.
    - Put 1 life saver on the yarn and tie a knot.

3. Tie the 'rosary necklace' to the cross section. Use tape if necessary and clip off any excess yarn. The rosary beads are now complete!

Other Ideas:

1. Another craft for this lesson could be to create a Prayer Book page using the "Hail Mary" prayer. Follow the directions for the Annunciation craft substituting the "Hail Mary" for the "Prayer to My Guardian Angel."

2. Use other various beads such as buttons or craft beads for the rosary.

3. Put each child's rosary in a zip-lock plastic bag for a rosary case.

The Nativity
Luke 2:1-7

Memory Verse:
"She gave birth to her first-born son and wrapped him in swaddling clothes, and laid him in a manger, because there was no room for them in the inn."
(Luke 2:7)

Joseph was engaged to be married to the Virgin Mary. He was very confused and ashamed when he learned that Mary was already pregnant before they were married. But, an angel of the Lord appeared to Joseph and told him to take Mary into his home and care for her, because the Father of Jesus is God. St. Joseph would be the foster father of Jesus.

In those days, Caesar August called for a census. Joseph and Mary had to leave their home in Nazareth to go to Bethlehem. They were very tired and Mary was expecting to give birth to her baby very soon. Joseph knocked on doors and asked people to rent them a room for the night. But everyone turned them away. Nobody had any room for Joseph and Mary.

Joseph didn't know what to do! One man let Joseph take Mary into his barn for the night. Animals made the barn smelly, but at least it was warm. Joseph got some fresh, clean straw for Mary to lie down on. Mary was far away from home and her family. She had never had a baby before and had no one there to help her. Most women have a mother or sister or doctor to help them deliver their first baby. Mary gave birth to baby Jesus and wrapped him in swaddling clothes, making a bed for baby Jesus in the manger.

This was the first Christmas. Mary gave birth to baby Jesus, her first and only son, the Son of God. He is the Savior of the World come to take away our sin and make things right with God the Father. Mary is the Mother of God and the mother of Christians. We call her our "Blessed Mother."

If you had been in Bethlehem, would you have made room for Joseph and Mary? God is happy when we make room for the traveler among us. You can make room for Jesus and Mary and Joseph right now. You can make room for Jesus to live in your heart. Do you know any Christmas carols? Some Christmas songs, like "Silent Night" and "Away in a Manger" tell the whole Christmas story. Sing a Christmas carol right now. Then tell the whole Christmas story to a friend in your own words.

The Nativity

Nativity Craft

This craft will make a manger with baby Jesus covered in a colorful blanket.

Materials:

brown and white construction paper, raffia for hay, tape or glue sticks, cardboard from empty toilet paper rolls, tissues, markers, scissors

Preparation:

1. Cut a piece of brown construction paper in half (short sides together).

2. Then fold and cut these pieces in half again (short sides together). Each manger will be comprised of two of these small rectangles and one full piece of brown construction paper.

3. Trace and cut a small circle (2.5" in diameter) for baby Jesus' head.

Assembling:

1. *To make the manger:*

   • Draw vertical lines with dark crayon or marker down from the short end of the construction paper to the other short end. This will give the paper a 'wood-like' look. Don't forget to draw these lines on the small pieces of paper, which are the legs of the manger.

- Fold this large piece of construction paper in half (short sides together) with the drawn lines on the outside.

- Carefully cut two slits about 4 inches in length on the fold 2.5 inches from each end.

- Place the small pieces of paper into the slits of the folded paper, and then open up the folded paper to make a "V." This is now the manger.

2. *To make baby Jesus:*

- Draw a face on the small white circle.

- Glue the face to the toilet paper holder to make the baby.

3. Add a small amount of raffia to the manger for hay.

4. Place baby Jesus in the manger.

5. Create designs on one or two tissues using markers. When complete, place the beautiful blanket on baby Jesus to keep Him warm.

Other Ideas:

1. Glue white paper around the toilet paper roll for a cleaner look.

2. Make and glue arms to the baby Jesus.

3. Use construction paper or foam in place of the cardboard rolls.

The Shepherds and the Angels
Luke 2:8-20

Memory Verse:
"To you is born this day . . . a Savior who is Christ the Lord."
(Luke 2:11)

"And in that region there were shepherds out in the field, keeping watch over their flock by night. And an angel of the Lord appeared to them, and the glory of the Lord shone around them, and they were filled with fear. And the angel said to them, 'Be not afraid; for behold, I bring you good news of great joy which will come to all the people; for to you is born this day in the city of David a Savior, who is Christ the Lord. And this will be a sign for you: you will find a babe wrapped in swaddling clothes and lying in a manger.' And suddenly there was with the angel a multitude of the heavenly host praising God and saying,

'Glory to God in the highest, and on earth peace among men with whom He is pleased.'

When the angels went away from them into heaven, the shepherds said to one another, 'Let us go over to Bethlehem and see what the Lord has made known to us.' And they went with haste, and found Mary and Joseph, and the babe lying in a manger" (Luke 2:8-16).

The shepherds were poor people and their work was cold and dirty. Sheep smell stinky and often the shepherds would smell stinky, too. The shepherds were lonely on the hillside, watching their sheep. People didn't like the bad smell of the sheep and the poor shepherds. Shepherds didn't have many friends. Sometimes it got very cold at night while they protected the sheep from being attacked and eaten by wolves.

Have you ever been cold or afraid? Did you ever feel lonely or wish you had a friend? The angels came to bring good news to the shepherds. They told the shepherds that Jesus came for the poor and the lonely. Jesus came to be a friend to everyone. Jesus takes away our fear. When we love Jesus, we know that we are never alone. Ask Jesus to come into your heart. Thank Jesus for being your forever friend. Jesus will never leave you or disappoint you. Jesus is always watching over you and loving you.

If you had been in Bethlehem, would you have let the shepherds join in your play? We want to include everyone. Do you feel sad when someone doesn't want to play with you? Others feel sad when they are excluded and left out. Jesus never left anyone out. Jesus loved everybody.

Jesus is the Savior of the world and your Savior too!

The Shepherds and the Angels

Shepherds and Angels Craft

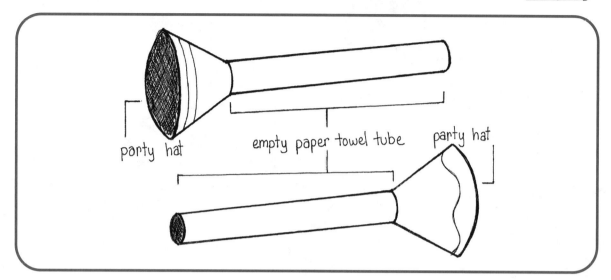

party hat   empty paper towel tube   party hat

This craft will make a decorative trumpet used to announce the birth of Christ. The children can celebrate with their trumpets singing "Hark the Herald Angels Sing."

Materials:
yellow construction paper, cardboard from paper towel rolls (1 per craft), plain birthday hats, glue, glue stick, tape, scissors, glitter, markers, crayons

Preparation:
1. Cut the tip off the birthday hats (about 1").

Assembling:
1. Insert the birthday hat into the paper towel tube and tape it in place.
2. Put glue on one side of the construction paper to wrap around the trumpet. Roll the paper towel tube over the construction paper to adhere together.
3. Put a line of glue around the rim of the "horn" part of the trumpet and sprinkle glitter on it. This will give the trumpet a "heavenly" look.
4. Decorate the horn with markers and crayons. The trumpet is now complete!
5. Dance, march and sing with the trumpets to "Hark the Herald Angels Sing."

Other Ideas:
1. Use construction paper instead of birthday hats. Fold in the shape of a hat; cut off tip and tape to paper towel tube.
2. Use funnel shape coffee filters instead of birthday hats.
3. Tape wax paper over the end of the trumpet (by the horn part) for a trumpet-like sound.
4. Use other decorative items to adorn the trumpets (buttons, bows, etc.).

The Magi
Matthew 2:1-12

Memory Verse:
"Where is the . . . king of the Jews?"
Matthew 2:2 (NAB)

When Jesus was born in Bethlehem in the manger, some wise men came from far away. These three kings went to Jerusalem on camels and asked King Herod where they could find the King of the Jews, for they had seen His star in the east. King Herod was jealous of Baby Jesus. He didn't want another king. He wanted to be the only king. Herod asked the wise men to come back and tell him where Baby Jesus was after they found Him, so he could worship, too.

The wise men looked up in the sky and kept on following the brilliant star, which led them to Bethlehem. These kings were very smart and studied hard. They had read that the Messiah would be born in Bethlehem. When the star led them to Jesus, they were filled with great joy! The wise men found Mary and Baby Jesus in the stable in Bethlehem. What an odd place for a king! They expected that a king would be born in a palace.

They bowed down and worshiped Jesus and gave Him gifts. They gave Jesus gold which shows that Jesus is the King of Kings! They gave Jesus frankincense to show that Jesus is the High Priest. They gave Jesus myrrh which is used for burial, because Jesus would die for the sins of the whole world.

The wise men show us that Jesus came to be the Savior of all the world. He came to save the rich and the poor, the learned kings and the simple shepherds. He came to save people at home and people in far away countries who have different colors of skin and speak foreign languages.

The kings were warned in a dream not to go back to King Herod, because Herod wanted to kill Baby Jesus. His soldiers killed all the baby boys. So, the wise men went back to their country by a different way.

Because the kings brought gifts to Baby Jesus, we give gifts at Christmastime too. What kind of present would you like to get at Christmas? What gifts can you give? If you had been in Bethlehem on the first Christmas, what present would you give to Baby Jesus? If you don't have a gift for Jesus, you can give Him your heart! That's the best gift of all!

The Magi

Magi Craft

This craft will allow the child to make a beautiful star Christmas ornament.

Materials:

small paper plates, hole puncher, BLUE crayons or markers, tape, yellow yarn, scissors

Preparation:

1. Punch a hole in the center of each small plate. In addition, punch 16 more holes randomly around the plate, which will become the points of the star.

2. Cut a piece of yarn 24" long. Tie a knot in one end and tape the other to allow for easing sewing.

Assembling:

1. Color the front of the paper plate with blue crayon or marker to create the night sky.

2. *Sew the star.*

  • Start at the back of the plate and come through the center hole.

  • Continue to sew by threading the yarn through a point hole and then through the back of the center hole. This will create the star look.

  • Knot the yarn on the back side of the plate and cut off any extra yarn when finished sewing.

3. Write on the back of the plate "WISE MEN STILL FOLLOW HIM." There should be room along the top for this.

4. Punch a hole at the top of the ornament and tie a small yarn hook through it. This will allow the ornament to be hung on a Christmas tree.

Other Ideas:

1. Use blue plates to eliminate coloring time.

2. Glue a paper star to the paper plate, eliminating sewing for younger children. The star can then be decorated with glue and glitter.

3. Add a splash of glitter to give the star a twinkling look.

4. Construction paper or foam can be used in place of the paper plate. This can be done by first gluing the paper to a frame made from four popsicle or craft sticks.

The Flight into Egypt
Matthew 2:13-23

After the wise men left Bethlehem to return to their own lands, an angel of the Lord appeared to Joseph in a dream. The angel told Joseph to take Mary and Baby Jesus to Egypt, because King Herod wanted to kill Baby Jesus. Joseph woke up right away. Joseph loved God and obeyed quickly. He took a donkey and put Mary and Baby Jesus on the donkey and hurried to the land of Egypt, where they would be safe.

When King Herod found out that the wise men had tricked him and gone back to their country by another road, he was furious. Now, King Herod knew that he was not the only king. In his furious rage, King Herod ordered his soldiers to kill all the baby boys under two years old in the land. That way he would kill the baby king and would be the only king once again. Soldiers killed the baby boys, and all the mothers and fathers were crying in the whole land.

But, because Joseph obeyed the angel, Mary and Jesus were safe in Egypt. When Herod died, an angel appeared to Joseph in another dream and told him that now it was safe to take Mary and Jesus back to the land of Israel. Joseph again obeyed.

He took Mary and Jesus to Galilee, to a town called Nazareth. Jesus was born in Bethlehem and grew up in Nazareth. That is why Jesus was called a Nazarene. But the prophet, Micah, foretold that the Savior would be born in Bethlehem. So Jesus was born in one place, Bethlehem, but grew up in another town, Nazareth.

Joseph was obedient to God. He loved Jesus and Mary and took good care of them. St. Joseph is the patron saint of families. Joseph was a carpenter who made tables and chairs for people. He was a very good carpenter and Joseph taught Jesus how to be a good carpenter, too. Carpenters work with hammers and nails, saws and boards to build useful things. Can you build things? Does your Daddy or Grandpa build things for you?

We want to be obedient to God, just like St. Joseph was obedient to God. One way to be obedient to God is to obey Mommy and Daddy. When they ask you to do something, do it right away. Obey quickly. Do not delay. What can you do to obey Mommy and Daddy more quickly?

 # Flight into Egypt Craft

JOSEPH IS
GLUED ON
THE CLOTHESPIN

The children can make a standing donkey to carry Mary and baby Jesus to Egypt with Joseph walking alongside the donkey.

Materials:

clothes pins that pinch open and shut, picture of Jesus, Mary and Joseph (use the illustration from this lesson), scissors, glue, crayons or markers

Preparation:

1. Remove the illustration of "The Flight into Egypt" from the book.

Assembling:

1. Color the picture of Jesus, Mary and Joseph and the donkey.

2. Cut out the picture of Mary holding Jesus on the donkey in one piece. Then cut out Joseph as a separate piece.

3. Cut the legs off the donkey and clip two clothes pins to where the legs would be, front and back. The donkey should now be able to stand on its own.

4. Glue Joseph to a clothespin, pinched side up, so that he can stand also.

5. Craft is complete. Children can pretend to move the donkey and Joseph to Egypt.

Other Ideas:

1. Glue Joseph directly onto the donkey if no clothespin is available.

2. Use pipe cleaners instead of clothespins.

The Presentation
Luke 2:21-40

Mary and Joseph took Baby Jesus to the temple in Jerusalem to present Him to the Lord, as God had commanded. They brought a sacrifice to offer to the Lord in thanksgiving for the birth of this healthy baby boy. The law of the Lord indicated that they should bring a pair of turtledoves or two young pigeons. That was the gift that poor people offered and Joseph and Mary were poor. So, that is what they did.

Now, in the temple there was an old man named Simeon. Simeon was a good and godly man. He prayed in the temple and hoped for the coming of the Messiah. God promised Simeon that he would not die before he had seen the Lord's Christ with his own eyes. Simeon prayed and prayed for God to send a savior for Israel.

One day, the Holy Spirit prompted Simeon to go to the temple. When he arrived, he saw Joseph and Mary bringing Baby Jesus to the temple. When Simeon saw Baby Jesus, he was so happy. He took Baby Jesus in his arms and thanked God and said:

"Lord, now let your servant depart in peace,

for my eyes have seen your salvation

a light for revelation to the Gentiles,

and for glory to your people Israel."

Luke 2:29-31

Anna, a very old lady who loved God, was also in the temple. She prayed and prayed. When she saw Jesus, she also gave thanks to God.

Simeon then told Mary that a sword would pierce her heart. The Blessed Mother would have many sorrows in her life. She would see Jesus suffer and die for our sins. That is why we call Mary, Our Lady of Sorrows.

When you were a baby, your parents brought you to church and thanked God for you, too. Your parents and god-parents brought you to the priest and asked for the sacrament of Baptism for you. You were given the sacrament which took away the stain of original sin, so you could be a child of God, and come into the family of God in the Catholic Church. Do you know your godparents? Ask Mommy and Daddy to tell you who your godparents are. Pray for them.

The Presentation

The Presentation Craft

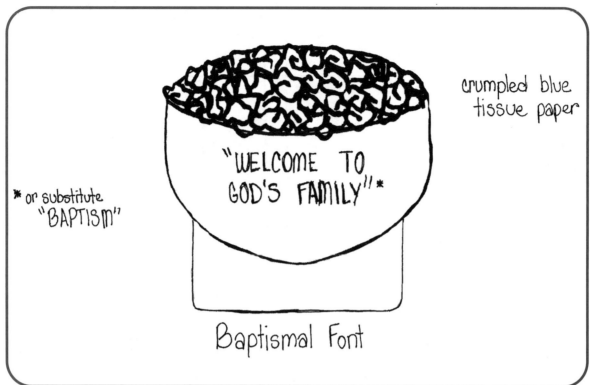

crumpled blue tissue paper

"WELCOME TO GOD'S FAMILY"*

* or substitute "BAPTISM"

Baptismal Font

This craft will make a Baptismal font using construction paper and tissue paper for holy water. Use this craft to teach the Sign of the Cross, since you are baptized in the name of the Father, Son and the Holy Spirit.

Materials:

yellow heavy stock construction paper, light blue tissue paper, glue, scissors, crayons

Preparation:

1. Trace and cut a Baptismal font to use as a pattern. Make a large half oval or circle with a rectangular bottom.

2. Cut 30 small pieces of tissue paper approximately 3" x 3" in size for each craft.

Assembling:

1. Trace the pattern of the Baptismal font on the yellow construction paper. Cut out the Baptismal font.

2. Trace an inside rim on the Baptismal font. Do this by connecting the tip of one side of the font to the other with an arch-shape.

3. Crumple up each small piece of tissue paper and glue it to the inside of the font to look like water.

4. Write on the font "Welcome to God's Family" or "Baptism."

5. Pretend a Baptism using the craft and a hand scooping the water in the name of the Father, Son and Holy Spirit.

Other Ideas:

1. Use poster paper instead of construction paper for the Baptismal font.

2. Use paper bowls as the Baptismal font instead of making one from paper.

3. Teach the Sign of the Cross to the children while making the craft.

The Finding in the Temple
Luke 2:41-52

Jesus, Mary and Joseph went up to the temple in Jerusalem for Passover every year. It was a big feast and celebration for the Jewish people.

When Jesus was twelve years old, Jesus, Mary and Joseph went up to the temple for the feast of Passover, as was their custom. Many relatives, friends and people from their town went also. It was a very long journey, taking several days of walking and camping out at night. Sometimes Jesus and the other children would run ahead and then wait for their parents to catch up with them. It was lots of fun.

When they got to the temple, Jesus sat with the teachers and asked them questions. The priests and teachers were amazed at Jesus' understanding.

Meanwhile, Joseph and Mary packed their belongings and started the long walk back to Nazareth. Mary walked with her aunts and cousins and women friends. Joseph was busy talking to the men as they walked.

Mary thought that Jesus was with Joseph, while Joseph thought that Jesus was with His mother. But, Jesus was lost! They were so worried! Have you ever been lost?

Joseph and Mary walked back to the temple in Jerusalem, searching for Jesus. They looked and looked and asked everyone if they had seen Jesus. When they got to the temple, there was Jesus sitting with the elders!

Mary said, "Son, your father and I have been looking for you. We were so afraid."

Jesus said, "Why did you look for Me? Didn't you know that I must be in My Father's house?" Jesus tells us that He is both the Son of God and the Son of Mary. The temple is God's house. Jesus is true God and true man. That is why Jesus can take away our sins and make things right between man and God the Father.

Jesus went back to Nazareth with Joseph and Mary and was obedient to them. Jesus increased in wisdom.

Jesus knew that He was God. Jesus chose to be obedient to His mother and His foster-father, Saint Joseph. God is happy when we are obedient to our parents, too. On Sunday, we go to church, which is God's house. How do we behave when we go into God's house? Do you know how to genuflect and sit nicely in God's house? Do you listen to the priest and sing the songs? Would you like to sing a song to God right now?

The Finding in the Temple

The Finding in the Temple Craft

The children can make temple doors, that, when opened, will show a colorful picture of Jesus teaching in the temple.

Materials:

picture of Jesus teaching in the temple from the lesson, construction paper, crayons or markers, glue, scissors

Preparation:

1. Remove the illustration, "The Finding in the Temple," from the book.

Assembling:

1. Color the picture of Jesus teaching in the temple from the illustration.

2. Cut any excess writing off the picture so only the illustration is showing.

3. Glue the colored picture in the center of a piece of construction paper.

4. Fold the picture in half, connecting the left to the right side, and open it up.

5. Fold the left and right side of the picture in to meet at the center fold. This will create a door.

6. Decorate the temple door with crayons or markers. Make a door knob and windows if you like.

7 The craft is complete! When the temple doors are opened, Jesus will be teaching. This craft will be able to stand up too!

Other Ideas:

1. Glue tiny pieces of colored paper in the windows of the temple doors to give a stained glass look.

2. Cut Jesus out of the illustration and glue Him to a Popsicle stick to make a puppet-like Jesus teaching in the temple.

The Baptism of the Lord
Mark 1:9-11

John the Baptist was the cousin of Jesus. Mary's cousin, Elizabeth, and Zechariah the high priest, were the parents of John. When John and Jesus grew up, John lived in the wilderness of Judea. John wore camel's hair for his clothing and he ate locusts and wild honey. He warned people to stop sinning and turn to God.

Sometimes people would confess their sins and John would baptize them in the River Jordan. John the Baptist was the messenger of the Lord, preparing the way for Jesus to come. John said "Someone is following me, someone who is more powerful than I am, and I am not fit to kneel down and undo the strap of his sandals. I have baptized you with water, but he will baptize you with the Holy Spirit" (Mark 1:7-8 JB)

One day, John saw Jesus coming toward him. John said "Behold, the Lamb of God, who takes away the sin of the world"(John 1:29). John knew that Jesus would be the perfect, sacrificial Passover Lamb that could take away all our sins.

Jesus asked John the Baptist to baptize Him. John was confused. John knew that he needed Jesus to baptize him and not the other way around, but he obeyed Jesus.

When John the Baptist baptized Jesus in the Jordan River, the heavens opened and the Spirit of God, like a dove, descended and hovered above Jesus. A voice from heaven said "This is my beloved Son, with whom I am well pleased" (Matthew 3:17).

In this way, everyone could see that Jesus was the only Son of God the Father. This event gives us a picture of the Blessed Trinity. We see God the Father, Jesus and the Holy Spirit. This is the truth of our faith. We believe in one God in three Divine persons. We profess this faith and proclaim it when we make the "Sign of the Cross."

Do you know how to make the "Sign of the Cross?" Your teacher will help you. Press your right thumb, index finger and middle finger all together tightly.

✛ Touch your forehead with your right three fingers and say

"In the name of the Father........"

✛ Touch your chest, with those three fingers, and say

"and of the Son....."

✛ Cross to your left shoulder and back to your right shoulder,

saying *"and of the Holy Spirit, Amen."*

Next Sunday, when you go into church, dip your fingers in the Holy Water font with your right hand, genuflect on your right knee, and make the sign of the cross. In this way, you face the tabernacle, where God lives. Can you find the tabernacle light that shows that Jesus is present? What color is the candle?

Genuflecting and making the sign of the cross show God that we love Him and want to live for Him. These gestures show our respect for God.

Even though you are small, you can talk to God. Close your eyes and say, "I love you, God. Please watch over me."

You should be very good in church. Being quiet and listening in Mass will help you to get to know God better. Are you a very good listener in Church?

Boys and girls who make noise in church make it hard for others to pray and pay attention. When you are quiet and pray to God, others can pray better, too. In this way we show respect for God and consideration for others.

Baptism of the Lord Craft

This craft will make a beautiful picture of Jesus being baptized and show how the Holy Spirit may have come down (as a stick-puppet) upon Jesus.

Materials:

picture of Jesus being baptized (use illustration with lesson on the preceding page), craft sticks or Popsicle sticks, crayons or markers, glue, glitter, scissors

Preparation:

1. Remove the illustration, "Baptism of Jesus," from the book and make a copy of it.

2. Cut a line from the top of Jesus' head to the clouds using scissors on one of the illustrations. The other illustration will be used to cut out the Holy Spirit dove to be used as a puppet.

Assembling:

1. Color the slit illustration of Jesus being baptized with crayons and markers.

2. Put glue along the lines from the cloud to Jesus and sprinkle glitter over the glue to give a spectacular look.

3. Cut out the picture of the Holy Spirit dove from the other illustration. Glue the dove to the craft stick so when the stick is horizontal, the dove is flying.

4. Craft is complete. Move the Holy Spirit puppet to show how God sent the Holy Spirit down upon Jesus from the Heavens above.

Other Ideas:

1. Glue glitter on the dove for a more majestic look.

2. Glue cotton balls to the clouds.

3. Glue the colored illustration to a piece of cardboard or construction paper to make it sturdier. Don't forget to cut the slit into the construction paper too.

Jesus' Temptation
Matthew 4:1-11

After Jesus was baptized in the Jordan River, by John the Baptist, the Spirit led Jesus into the wilderness. Jesus prayed and fasted for forty days and forty nights. Afterward, Jesus was very hungry and very thirsty.

The devil came up to Jesus to tempt Him. The devil, also called Satan or the evil one, was once an angel who refused to obey God. St. Michael the Archangel cast Satan out of heaven and thrust him into hell. The devil didn't want Jesus to die for our sins, so we could go to heaven. Satan is jealous of us, because we are made in the image and likeness of God. Now Satan tries to lie and tempt people to sin. The evil one doesn't want us to be good and go to heaven to live with God forever at the end of our lives.

Jesus was hungry. The tempter told Jesus to turn stones into bread, if He was the Son of God. Jesus knew the word of God in the scriptures and said "It is written: 'Man doesn't live by bread alone, but by every word that comes from the mouth of God'" (Matthew 4:4).

Then the devil took Jesus to the very top of the temple and told Jesus to throw Himself down and ask the angels to catch Him. Jesus said "You shall not tempt the Lord your God" (Matthew 4:7).

Finally, Satan took Jesus to a high mountain and showed Him all the kingdoms of the world. Satan wanted Jesus to worship him! But, Jesus wouldn't do it. Jesus said "You shall worship the Lord your God and him only shall you serve" (Matthew 4:10).

Then the devil went away from Jesus and left Him alone and the angels of God came and took care of Jesus, bringing Him food and drink.

Always remember to love God and God alone. Everyday tell Jesus you love Him. Call on Jesus when you are in trouble and He will comfort you. You have a guardian angel who watches over you to protect you from evil. Remember to pray to your guardian angel every day. Never dabble in evil. Avoid places where you may be tempted. Do not read books about witches or demons or anything from the kingdom of darkness. Always live in the kingdom of light. Always ask God to allow you to remain in a state of grace.

Do you know this prayer to St. Michael the archangel?

Prayer to St. Michael the Archangel

St. Michael the Archangel,

defend us in battle.

Be our safeguard

against the wickedness

and snares of the devil.

May God rebuke him we humbly pray,

and do thou

O Prince of the Heavenly Host,

by the power of God,

cast into Hell Satan

and all the evil spirits

who prowl about the world

seeking the ruin of souls.

Amen.

If you are ever afraid or in trouble, pray to your guardian angel and St. Michael. If you are tempted by the devil, call on the name of Jesus and Satan will go away. Pray: "Jesus, My Lord and My God, I trust in You." Remember, Jesus is the Victor!

Jesus' Temptation

Jesus is Tempted Craft

This craft will produce a decorative prayer book that when opened will display the "Prayer to St. Michael the ArchAngel." (Note, if a prayer book has already been made by the child, simply add this prayer.)

Materials:

colorful foam paper, hole puncher, yarn, markers, glue, scissors, tape, stickers (optional), "Prayer to St. Michael the Archangel" printed on paper 4" x 6"

Preparation:

1. Fold and cut each piece of foam paper in half, short sides together.

2. Punch holes around the rim of the foam paper.

3. Pre-print or type the "St. Michael the Archangel" prayer on paper for each craft.

4. Cut two 24" pieces of yarn and one 10" piece of yarn for each craft. Tie a knot at the end and put tape around the tip of the other side for ease of sewing.

Assembling:

1. Using markers, write "MY PRAYER BOOK" in the center of one piece of pre-punched foam paper. Be sure to hold the foam paper short side on top.

2. Decorate the cover of the prayer book with stickers or markers.

3. Thread the yarn in and out of the holes all the way around the foam paper. Tie a knot and cut off excess when you reach the first hole. Repeat this for the other piece of foam paper.

4. Place the two foam pieces together, making the book and punch two new holes in the center left side approximately 2-3 inches from each other.

5. Thread the small piece of yarn through the two holes, starting from the back. Tie a knot and a bow in the front to bind the book together.

6. Open the book and write "Prayer to St. Michael the Archangel" on the inside cover.

7. Glue the pre-printed copy of the St. Michael the Archangel prayer on the facing page and the prayer book is now complete!

Other Ideas:

1. Use paper plates, poster paper or felt instead of foam paper.

2. Use other decorations such as buttons, fabric, foil, pompoms, religious pictures cut from greeting cards, holy cards or stickers to beautify the cover of the book.

3. Use glitter blue markers for writing "MY PRAYER BOOK" for a puffy and fancy look.

4. Add more pages with more prayers if time allows.

5. Use ribbon instead of yarn for binding the pages together.

Jesus Teaches

Sermon on the Mount
Matthew 5:1-16

One day Jesus went up on a mountain. When He sat down, His disciples came to Him and Jesus began to teach them. Jesus said,

"Happy are the poor in spirit,
 for theirs is the kingdom of God.
 Happy are those who are sad,
 for they will be comforted.
Happy are the meek and humble,
 for they will inherit the earth.
Happy are those who hunger for righteousness,
 for they will be satisfied.
Happy are the kind and merciful,
 for they will receive mercy.
Happy are the pure in heart,
 for they will see God.
Happy are the peacemakers,
 they will be called children of God.
Happy are those who suffer for righteousness' sake,
 for theirs is the kingdom of heaven.
Happy are you when others say bad things about you
 because you love God.
Rejoice and be glad,
 for your reward in heaven will be great!"

(Matthew 5:3-12)

Jesus taught the disciples that bad things would happen. People say mean things and hurt other people. People get hurt and get sick. Soldiers would beat and crucify Jesus. Some of the apostles would be killed because of their love for Jesus. But, Jesus promised that even if bad things happen in this world, we should keep thinking about how wonderful heaven will be.

Jesus wants us to be good and humble, kind and forgiving. Fighting and saying bad words and calling people names make God sad. God wants us to be friends with others, to share what we have and to be kind. He wants us to talk nice. We must never make fun of other people, especially if they look different from us. Some people have a different color skin, or walk with a limp or sit in a wheelchair. God loves them, too. We must try to be kind to everyone. We pray for everyone.

Sometimes we hurt people by accident. We might bump into someone, while running in the park. Right away we help the other person and tell him we are sorry and ask if he is all right. If someone hurts you and says he is sorry, forgive him.

Forgiveness is very important to learn. Try to practice this right now. Go to your friend, next to you and say "I'm sorry. Please forgive me." Your friend should say, "I forgive you." Then you shake hands or give a hug and everyone feels better.

Grown-ups need to learn to be peacemakers, too. Mommies and daddies sometimes need to say "I'm sorry. Please forgive me." Then they hear "I forgive you. I love you." Soon it gets all better. That makes God happy.

When we learn to be humble, to say we're sorry, to ask forgiveness and offer forgiveness, we become like Jesus. We make God very happy. And God makes us happy. Our light shines in the darkness and people know we are Christians by our love for one another.

What could you do to be kind and forgiving to another person? How can you make God happy?

Have you ever done something wrong and asked forgiveness? Has anyone ever done something wrong to you and asked your forgiveness?

Love means learning to forgive and to ask forgiveness.

Sermon on the Mount

 # Sermon on the Mount Craft

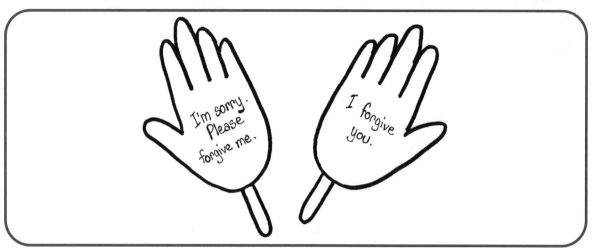

This craft will make two hand puppets that can shake hands and can be used to teach children about forgiveness.

Materials:

craft sticks or Popsicle sticks, construction paper, crayons or markers, glue, pencil, scissors

Preparation:

1. Trace and cut a pattern of an adult size left hand print and a right hand print (fingers closed with thumb up).

Assembling:

1. Fold one piece of construction paper in half and cut.
2. Trace and cut a "left" hand print. Write "I'm sorry. Please forgive me" in the palm of the left hand using crayons or markers.
3. Trace and cut a "right" hand print. Write "I Forgive You" in the palm of the right hand using crayons or markers.
4. Glue the hands to the craft stick so that the writings will be showing. The back of both thumbs should line up as well as the finger tips.
5. Have the children practice shaking hands with each other saying "I'm sorry. Please forgive me" and then other responding "I Forgive You."

Other Ideas:

1. Make separate puppets for each saying. Each child could then practice at home.
2. Decorate the fingers and hands of the craft by drawing rings, finger nails, a watch or bracelet.

The Lord's Prayer
Matthew 6:9-13

Jesus loved to take time away to pray to His Father in heaven. We want to be like Jesus. We want to do what He did. Prayer is talking to God and listening to God. Whenever you are frightened or in need, you can pray to your Father in Heaven and He will hear you. When you wake up in the morning and when you go to sleep at night, pray and ask God to watch over you.

Jesus' disciples wanted to know how to pray better. So, they asked Jesus to teach them how to pray. Jesus told them that they didn't need to use a lot of fancy words. God, the Father knows all things. He already knows what we need, even before we ask Him. Jesus warned us not to make a big deal about praying or to try to impress other people and show off. Jesus said to go to our room and pray simply. God likes simple prayers. Jesus said to pray like this.

The Lord's Prayer

Our Father, who art in heaven,

Hallowed be Thy name.

Thy kingdom come.

Thy will be done, on earth as it is in heaven.

Give us this day our daily bread;

And forgive us our trespasses,

As we forgive those who trespass against us;

And lead us not into temptation,

But deliver us from evil.

Amen.

Can you pray The Lord's Prayer? We also call this prayer "The Our Father." Pray this prayer right now. If you pray this prayer every Sunday in Mass, soon you will know it by heart.

Ask Mommy and Daddy to pray this prayer with you.

When you are bigger, you will learn many beautiful prayers. Just now, you can pray by just talking to God in your own words. When you pray, you can do many different things and talk to God in different ways.

- **Adore God** - Tell God how wonderful He is, how good He is, how beautiful His creation is.

- **Confess your sins** - Tell God you are sorry for all your sins. Promise God you will try, with His help, to be better.

- **Thank God for everything** - Thank God for life, for your Mommy and Daddy, Grandma and Grandpa, brothers and sisters. Thank God for your house and your bed, for your warm clothes and good food. What else can you thank God for?

- **Ask God for what you need** - Remember to pray for your needs as well as the needs of others in the world.
  Please God, feed the hungry children in the world.
  Please God, comfort the sick and dying.
  Please God, be with our Holy Father in Rome.
  Please God, bless your priests and send us more holy
      priests to bring us the sacraments.
  Please God bless Mommy and Daddy.

The Lord's Prayer

The Lord's Prayer Craft

This craft will produce a decorative prayer book that when opened will read "The Lord's Prayer." (Note: If the child has already made a prayer book with the lesson from the "Annunciation" or "Jesus is Tempted" chapters, this prayer can be simply inserted into or added to that prayer book.)

Materials:

colorful foam paper, hole puncher, yarn, markers, stickers (optional), glue, scissors, tape, "The Lord's Prayer" printed on 4" x 6" paper

Preparation:

1. Fold and cut each piece of foam paper in half (short sides together). Each craft will need one piece of foam paper.

2. Punch holes around the rim of the foam paper.

3. Pre-print or type the Lord's Prayer on paper. This can be done by printing two prayers per sheet of 8 1/2" x 11" paper on your computer using landscape mode. One prayer per child will be needed.

4. Cut 24" lengths of yarn (two per craft). Tie a knot at the end of each piece and place tape around the tip of the other end for ease of sewing.

5. Cut 10" pieces of yarn (one per craft). This will be used as the book's binding.

Assembling:

1. Write "MY PRAYER BOOK" using markers in the center of one piece of pre-punched foam paper. Be sure to hold foam paper short side on top.

2. Decorate the cover of the prayer book with stickers or markers.

3 Thread the yarn in and out of the holes all the way around the foam paper. Tie a knot and cut off the excess when you reach the first hole. Repeat this process for the other piece of foam paper.

4. Place the two foam pieces together (making the book) and punch two new holes in the center left side approximately 2-3 inches from each other.

5. Thread the small piece of yarn through the two holes, starting from the back. Tie a knot and then a bow in the front to bind the book together.

6. Open the book and write "LUKE 11:2-4" on the inside cover.

7. Glue the pre-printed copy of "The Lord's Prayer" on the facing page. The prayer book is now complete!

Other Ideas:

1. Use paper plates or poster paper instead of foam paper if not available.

2. Use other various decorations such as buttons, small pompoms, old puzzle pieces, stickers, holy pictures, cut up greeting cards or foil stars to adorn the cover of the prayer book. Extra time would need to be allowed for gluing these materials on the cover.

3 Use glitter glue markers for writing "MY PRAYER BOOK" for a puffy and fancy look.

4. Add more pages with more prayers if time allows ("The Sign of the Cross," "Glory Be to the Father," "Hail Mary," "Act of Contrition," or "Grace Before Meals.")

5. Use ribbon instead of yarn for binding the pages together.

Jesus Brings a Girl Back to Life
Mark 5:35-43

Jesus loves little children. Sometimes the grown-ups would try to make the children go away and leave Jesus alone because Jesus was very busy and sometimes He got tired. But, Jesus said, "Let the children come to me, do not hinder them; for to such belongs the kingdom of God. Truly, I say to you, whoever does not receive the kingdom of God like a child shall not enter it" (Mark 10:14-15).

Children trust that their parents will love and care for them. Daddy works hard. Mommy buys groceries and makes good food to eat. Just as we trust our earthly parents to take care of us, we must trust that God knows what is best for us. God will never leave us or neglect us.

One time a ruler of the synagogue, named Jairus came to Jesus. Jairus fell down at Jesus' feet and begged Jesus to come with him. Jairus said "My little daughter is at the point of death. (Please), come and lay your hands on her, so that she may be made well, and live" (Mark 5:23).

Jesus was sad for Jairus and agreed to go with him to his house to pray for the little girl. Along the way, a great crowd of people followed Jesus. A lady, who had been bleeding for a long time touched the hem of Jesus' garment and was healed. People could see that Jesus had power to make sick people get well again. Jesus helped blind people to see and made lame people walk. Everyone was amazed to see these wonders.

When Jesus arrived at Jairus' house, he learned that the little girl had already died. Was Jesus too late to heal her? The neighbors told Jairus not to bother Jesus anymore because his daughter was dead. But Jesus said "Do not fear, only believe" (Mark 5:36).

All of the friends and relatives were outside crying loudly because the little twelve year old girl they loved had died. Jesus told the people that the girl was not dead but only asleep. The people laughed at Jesus. They knew that dead was dead!

Jesus took Peter, James and John and the little girl's mother and father into the dead child's room with Him. Jesus took the girl by the hand and said "Talitha cum", which means "Little girl, get up." Immediately the little girl came to life and got up and walked around. Her parents were overjoyed. The apostles were astounded. The townspeople were incredulous.

Who has the power to raise the dead to life? Only God has power over life and death. Most people are afraid to die. We don't want to see our grandparents die and we don't want to die ourselves. It can be frightening. But Jesus shows us we don't need to be afraid of sickness or death. Jesus is always with us.

We want to die like Saint Joseph must have died, with Jesus and Mary by his side. That is why we pray that Jesus and Mary will be with us at the hour of our death to take us to heaven. Do you know this prayer?

Hail Mary

Hail Mary, full of grace,
The Lord is with thee,
Blessed art thou among women
And blessed is the fruit of thy womb, Jesus.

Holy Mary, Mother of God,
Pray for us sinners,
Now and at the hour of our death.
Amen.

Jesus Brings a Girl Back to Life

Jesus Brings a Girl Back to Life Craft

This craft will make the face of a little girl whose eyes are covered by her hands (showing that she is dead), and when her hands are opened the girl will be alive and well.

Materials:

paper plates, light colored construction paper, hair colored yarn (yellow, black, brown or orange), crayons or markers, glue, tape, scissors, pencil

Preparation:

1. Pre-cut 8" pieces of yarn and then tie a bunch together in the middle to create hair.

Assembling:

1. Draw a face on the paper plates. Have each child color the eyes the same color as his or her own.

2. Glue the yarn hair to the top of the plate using a color of yarn that resembles the child's own hair color. Cut off any excess hair length.

3. Fold a piece of construction paper in half. Trace the child's hand print by first placing the wrist on the fold and spreading the fingers wide. Cut the traced hand print out (there will be two attached hand prints) and then cut the hands apart.

4   Place each hand over one eye, fingertips facing each other. Tape them in place along the side of the plate. Hands will now be able to fold open and close like peek-a-boo.

5   Close the hands and write on the left closed hand "TALITHA" and on the right closed hand "CUM".

Other Ideas:

1. Cut out holes where the eyes are and tape a craft stick to the back of the plate, creating a hand-held mask. Let the children place the masks in front of their faces.

2. Use other craft materials: buttons, felt or sparkles to decorate the face on the plates.

Jesus Feeds Five Thousand
John 6

The people were very hungry. Andrew told Jesus that a little boy had five loaves of bread and two little fishes. The boy gave his lunch to Jesus to feed the people. Jesus was happy to accept the boy's lunch. Jesus took the bread, gave thanks to His Father in heaven and gave the food to the people.

Five thousand men plus women and children were sitting on the hillside listening to Jesus. When everyone finished eating, Jesus told the disciples to pick up the leftover food. Jesus didn't want to waste any of the food. The disciples gathered up twelve baskets of food. It was a miracle! There were more leftovers than there was food to start with.

One little boy shared his food and Jesus multiplied the food for the people. Jesus is happy when we give our heart to Him. He is happy when we share what we have with others. Do you know how to share? When did someone share something with you? Does it make you happy when you share with others? It makes God happy, too.

Jesus Feeds Five Thousand Craft

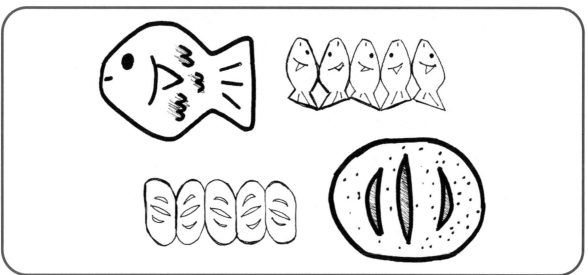

The children can make a craft that will visually show how Jesus fed five thousand people with just five loaves and two fishes. The loaves and fish will open up like paper-dolls displaying many leftovers.

Materials:

plastic fruit baskets (one per craft), crayons or markers, pencil, scissors, paper clips, brown/tan and yellow/orange construction paper

Preparation:

1. Fold construction paper into three equal strips (length ways) and cut strips apart. Repeat this step for the dark (brown/tan) and light (yellow/orange) construction paper. One light and one dark strip will be needed per craft.

Assembling:

1. *To make the fish:*

   • Take a strip of the light construction paper and fold the short side down in 2" folds. Repeat folding in an accordion fashion.

   • Trace a fish on the front fold touching all sides.

• Cut the traced fish out, being careful to not cut along the edges. This will allow the fish to open up like a paper doll.

• Open up the fish and make eyes and mouths on each fish.

• Fold the fish back up and paper clip the tail together to make one fish.

• Place in the basket.

2. *To make the loaves of bread:*

   • Take a strip of dark construction paper and fold the short side down in 2" folds. Repeat folding in an accordion fashion.

   • Trace a loaf of bread on the front fold touching all sides.

   • Cut the traced loaf out, being careful not to cut along the edges. This will allow the bread to open up like a paper doll.

   • Open up the bread and draw lines on each loaf to look like bread.

   • Fold the bread back up and paper clip together. Place in the basket.

3. Demonstrate what the little boy's lunch basket may have looked like and then show all the fish and bread that would have been left-over after Jesus blessed and shared with the five thousand people (remove the paper clips).

Other Ideas:

1. Skip making the bread and fish cutouts and just put goldfish crackers and breadsticks or saltine crackers (oyster crackers or graham crackers work well too!) in the basket to represent the fish and bread.

2. Weave ribbon or yarn through the basket to create a sharing basket.

3. Offer the children goldfish crackers and water for a snack. Bless the food before eating and talk about sharing, while the children eat.

Jesus Walks on Water
Luke 8:22-25

At nighttime, the disciples got into a boat and rowed across the lake. It was very dark. A strong wind was blowing and there were very big waves. When they had rowed three miles across the lake, they saw Jesus walking on the water. The disciples were frightened. They thought Jesus was a ghost! But Jesus said "It is I; do not be afraid" (John 6:20).

Peter wanted to walk on the water like Jesus. So Peter asked Jesus if he could come out and walk on the water, too. Jesus said "Yes." So, Peter got out and started walking on the water. But, then Peter took his eyes off Jesus. He looked down and got very scared and started sinking into the water. Jesus took Peter by the hand and helped him back into the boat.

Jesus fell asleep and a big storm came up on the lake. Big waves were crashing into the boat and water came onto the deck. The disciples ran to Jesus and woke him up. Jesus told the wind and the seas to calm down and be quiet and they did! The disciples were amazed to see that Jesus has authority over the forces of nature. They knew now that Jesus is God.

Jesus Walks on Water

Jesus Walks on Water Craft

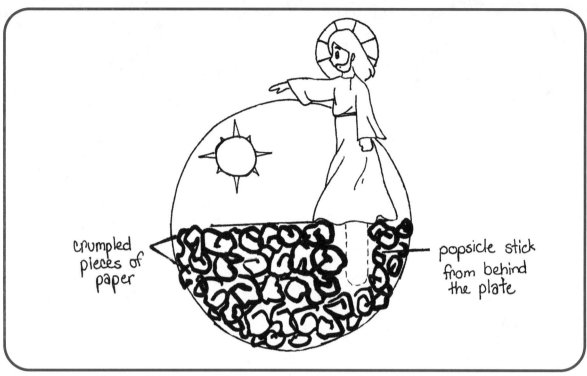

crumpled pieces of paper

popsicle stick from behind the plate

This craft will make a stick puppet of Jesus that walks on water.

Materials:

paper plates, craft sticks or Popsicle sticks, blue tissue paper, crayons, glue, scissors, picture of Jesus walking on the water (use illustration with lesson)

Preparation:

1. Cut a line in the center of a paper plate approximately 5" in length. This can be done by gently folding the plate in half, cutting and then releasing the plate as to not make a crease in the plate.

2. Remove the illustration, "Jesus Walks on the Water," from the book.

3. Pre-cut 3" x 3" pieces of blue tissue paper. Each craft will need 20-30 pieces.

Assembling:

1. Color the illustration of Jesus from of the lesson.

2. Cut out the silhouette of Jesus and glue Jesus to the craft stick. Set aside to dry.

3. Crumple up small pieces of tissue paper and glue to the paper plate below the cut line. Continue to do this until the bottom of the plate is completely covered with water.

4. Draw a sun on the top left of the plate.

5. Take the puppet of Jesus and put it through the slit of the paper plate starting from the back. Holding the plate in one hand and the puppet in the other, move Jesus along the water as though He is walking.

Other Ideas:

1. Use crayons or blue marker to color the water blue instead of using tissues.

2. Draw a boat, the disciples, sun, birds and so on using crayons above the water on the paper plate.

The Bread of Life
John 6:35-70

Memory Verse
**"I am the living bread which came down from heaven;
if (you) eat this bread, (you) will live forever."**
(John 6:51)

Jesus said "I am the Bread of Life. He who comes to Me will never go hungry." Jesus said "If you eat My flesh and drink My blood, you will live forever and I will raise you up on the last day."

Jesus died on the cross for our sins on Good Friday. But, on Easter Sunday, Jesus rose from the dead and showed the disciples that He is alive! Jesus promised us that He would be with us always until the end of the world. He remains with us in the Blessed Sacrament. Jesus is really present body, blood, soul and divinity in Holy Communion. At Mass we offer bread and wine to the priest. The priest offers the bread and wine to God. He prays the words of consecration and the bread and wine become the body and blood of Jesus! When will you be able to receive Holy Communion? What do children wear for their First Holy Communion? How can you get ready for it?

Thank you, Jesus, for the gift of the Eucharist.

The Bread of Life

The Bread of Life Craft

> The children can make a decorative tabernacle that opens up and shows the Eucharist, the bread of life.

Materials:

yellow construction paper (2 pieces per craft), white construction paper, glue sticks, gold glitter, scissors, markers or crayons

Preparation:

1. Trace and cut 3" diameter circles from white construction paper for a host.
2. Trace and cut a tabernacle from yellow construction paper (one per craft).
3. Lightly trace a large "T" in the bottom center of the tabernacle. This will be the door.
4. Fold and cut a second sheet of yellow construction paper in half, folding the short sides together. This will be in the inside of the tabernacle.

Assembling:

1. Carefully cut the "T" on the tabernacle and fold back the doors.
2. Glue the smaller yellow inside piece of paper behind the tabernacle. Be careful not to glue the doors shut.
3. Open the tabernacle doors and glue the host in the center.
4. Add sunshine rays around the host to show its splendor and write "The Bread of Life" across the top of the Eucharist.
5. Add glue swirls and designs on the front of the tabernacle and add glitter.
6. The tabernacle is finished! When the doors are open, the tabernacle should stand up on its own.

Other Ideas:

1. Use gold foil or glittery gold wrapping paper to decorate the tabernacle.
2. Use large raisin boxes or square Kleenex boxes for the tabernacle.

Jesus Works Miracles
John 11:1-57

One day, Jesus' friend, Lazarus, died. Lazarus' sisters, Martha and Mary, were so sad. Jesus went to see Martha and Mary to comfort them. Martha said "Lord, if you had been here, my brother would not have died. And even now I know that whatever you ask from God, God will give you." Jesus said to her, "Your brother will rise again" (John 11:21-23). Martha and Mary knew that one day their brother would rise to new life.

Jesus was sad that Lazarus was dead. Jesus cried for the loss of his friend Lazarus. Then Jesus went to the tomb where they had buried Lazarus and He told the people to move the stone. Martha was afraid that there would be a bad, bad smell, because Lazarus had been dead for three days.

Jesus insisted that the stone be rolled away. Then Jesus went to the tomb and lifted His eyes to heaven and prayed to God the Father in heaven. Then Jesus said "Lazarus, come out" (John 11:43). The dead man came out, all wrapped up in his burial clothes like a mummy. Jesus told the people to take the bandages off Lazarus so that he could go free.

Martha and Mary were so happy and grateful to God. All the people were amazed. Who is this that has the power to bring the dead back to life? Only God has power over life and death. In this way, the people knew that Jesus is really God.

What do you think would have happened if Jesus had not called Lazarus by name? Do you think that all of the dead people in the tombs would have come out? That is what will happen at the end of time. Jesus will call all of the dead people out of their tombs.

Do you know anyone who has died? When we get old, we will all get sick and die. Then we will stand before Jesus for judgment. We hope that when we die, Jesus will take us to heaven with Him. As Catholics we pray for those we love who have died. Do you know this prayer?

May all the souls of the faithful departed,
through the mercy of God
rest in peace.
Amen.

In our house, our Grandpa has died, and so we pray the prayer like this.

May Grandpa's soul
and all the souls of the faithful departed,
through the mercy of God
rest in peace.
Amen.

Jesus Works Miracles

 # Jesus Works Miracles Craft

The children can make stick puppets of Lazarus, Jesus, Martha and Mary which can be used to act out Jesus' miracle of raising Lazarus from the dead.

Materials:

picture of Lazarus (use illustration from the lesson), brown paper lunch bags, craft sticks or Popsicle sticks, crayons or markers, glue, scissors

Preparation:

Remove the Lazarus illustration from the book.

Assembling:

1. Color the picture of Jesus raising Lazarus from the dead with crayons.

2. Cut out each figure from the drawing and glue a craft stick to the back of each. Leave enough room on the bottom for a hand to hold the puppets.

3. Cut 4" off the open end of the lunch bag. The size of the bag should be equal to the length of Lazarus. The brown paper bag will be Lazarus' tomb.

4. Cut the tomb door out of the bag. Start at the open end of the bag and cut a large upside down "L" and then fold back the door.

5. Color the tomb using dark crayons for stones and rocks.

6. Act out the miracle starting with Lazarus in the tomb.

Other Ideas:

1. Use construction paper, old check boxes or square tissue boxes for the tomb.

2. Use clothespins instead of craft sticks for the puppets.

3. Create a shadow box of the miracle scene, using a shoe box, construction paper for the tomb and gluing the figures in the box.

Love One Another
John 15

Jesus taught His disciples and all the people who would listen to Him a whole new way to live. Jesus obeyed all the laws of God that were given to Moses. He obeyed the Ten Commandments. Do you know the Ten Commandments?

10 Commandments

1. Love God above all else. Don't worship false gods.
2. Don't take the name of the Lord in vain.
3. Keep holy the Lord's day.
4. Obey your father and your mother.
5. Do not kill.
6. Don't commit adultery.
7. Don't steal.
8. Don't lie.
9. Don't desire your neighbor's wife.
10. Don't long for your neighbor's goods.

Jesus loved and obeyed Mary and Joseph. He was good and obedient when He was a child. He did what He was asked to do quickly and cheerfully. Jesus prayed to God the Father and went to the temple. He was kind and good to people.

Jesus taught the disciples many things. Jesus gave us a brand new commandment. Jesus said "Love one another; even as I have loved you . . . By this all men will know that you are my disciples, if you have love for one another" (John 13:34-35).

Do you know how much Jesus loves you? He loves you so much that he went to the cross and died for your sins and the sins of the whole world. Even if you were the only person in the whole world, Jesus would have died just for you. That's how much He loves you.

The way that we love one another is to be kind and good to others. Share what you have with others. Speak kindly to others. Never make fun of other people, especially people who might look different. Never be mean or cruel or refuse to let others play. Never say bad words or call people bad names. Be concerned for the poor, the elderly, the handicapped. Always be kind and good and helpful to others.

Jesus said "Let your light so shine before men, that they may see your good works and give glory to your Father who is in heaven" (Matthew 5:16).

The early Christians did such a good job of loving and caring for one another that the pagans noticed. The pagans said "Look at how those Christians love one another." How can you show your love for others? How can you let your light shine?

Love One Another

 # Love One Another Craft

This craft will produce a love mobile that shows Jesus' new commandment and all the love He has for each and every one.

Materials:

pink, red, and light pink or purple construction paper, hole puncher, stapler, pink or purple string, crayons or markers, scissors

Preparation:

1. Trace and cut a heart about 5" x 5" in size to use as a pattern for hearts.

2. Cut string into 10" pieces (2 pieces per craft).

Assembling:

1. Trace two hearts on a red, pink and light pink piece of construction paper. Cut out 6 hearts in all, two of each color.

2. Assemble one red, pink and light pink heart into a pile and staple together in the center (staple should be vertical). Repeat for the remaining three hearts.

3. Punch a hole in the top center of both piles of hearts.

4. Punch a hole in the bottom point of ONE of the piles of hearts.

5. Fold the top heart in half and the bottom heart in half, creating a three-dimensional heart. Repeat this for the other stapled hearts.

6. Write a different saying on each of the hearts using crayons or markers:
   - Love One Another
   - As I Have Loved You
   - Be Kind
   - Be Helpful
   - Be Giving
   - Be Nice
   - Love Jesus
   - God Loves You
   - I Love You
   - Let Your Light Shine

7. Attach the string with knots to the top of both hearts. Connect the hearts together tying the string of one heart to the punched hole in the bottom of the other heart. The Love Mobile is complete! Watch it spin!

Other Ideas:

1. Decorate the hearts with glitter and glue instead of only markers.

2. In addition to writing the love sayings draw pictures of ways people can show they love each other.

3. Use ribbon or yarn instead of string to make the mobile.

Jesus Blesses Children
Luke 18:15-17

Once Jesus was teaching people about the kingdom of heaven. Many people gathered around to hear Jesus and to be near Him. Jesus often healed people who were sick. He put mud on a blind man's eyes and the blind man could see! Jesus put his fingers in the ears of a deaf man and opened his ears. For the first time, the man could hear laughter and singing and the voices of his loved ones. Once Jesus spoke to a man who had been crippled for many years. Jesus told the man to pick up his mat and walk. The man obeyed Jesus and walked around the temple. The man's parents knew that he had been crippled from birth. They were so happy to see their son well.

Leprosy was a very bad disease in Jesus' time. Lepers had to leave their homes and live outside of the town away from other people. Leprosy was a very contagious disease. If you touched a person with leprosy, you would become a leper yourself. No one would go near a leper. When people came near, the leper would cry out "Unclean, unclean." Then the people would run away. Jesus touched the lepers and cured them. They were so happy. They showed the priests that they were clean and then they returned to their families with great joy. Sometimes the people who were healed by Jesus were so happy that they forgot to say "Thank you" to Jesus. One day when Jesus healed ten lepers, nine of them forgot to come back and thank Jesus. Do you always remember to say "Thank you?"

Do you remember to thank Jesus for everything He gives you? Thank God every single day.

One day, mothers and fathers and grandmas and grandpas were bringing babies and children to Jesus. Some of the children were sick and some were healthy. The disciples were not happy. The disciples told the people not to bother Jesus with the children. But Jesus called the children to Him saying "Let the children come to me, and do not hinder them; for to such belongs the kingdom of God. Truly, I say to you, whoever does not receive the kingdom of God like a child shall not enter it" (Luke 18:16-17).

Jesus loves little children. God made you and breathed a soul into your body that will live forever. Jesus wants you to love Him and live for Him and spend all eternity with Him in heaven. Even when your mommy was carrying you in her body, under her heart, you had a living soul. God has known you for all time.

What do you think it means to receive the kingdom of God like a child? Children trust their parents to take care of them and protect them. Mommy and Daddy love you and take care of you. They make sure you have clothes to wear, good food to eat, toys to play with, and a warm house to live in.

God loves you and cares for you, too. God loves you even more than your parents do. You can trust God. He will always be with you. He will never leave you. When you are lonely or afraid, you can talk to God. Talking to God and listening to God is called prayer. Jesus invites little children to come to Him. Can you talk to Jesus in your own words? What would you like to say to Jesus? Tell Jesus how much you love Him. How many things can you think of to thank God for? Let's go around in a circle and thank God for all the things that can come into our minds.

Jesus Blesses Children

Jesus Blesses Children Craft

This craft will make a decorated frame which displays each child's hand prints with the verse: "Let the little children come to Me" Luke 18:16.

Materials:

Luke 18:16 printed on 8 1/2" x 11" paper, 8 1/2" x 11" manila folders, various colored foam paper, decorative materials (buttons, puzzle pieces, feathers, shiny decorative shapes), glue, water color paint, scissors, baby wipes or paper towels, soap, and water

Preparation:

1. Cut manila folders in half, using the crease as the cut mark.

2. Pre-print the following verse on 8 1/2" x 11" paper:

   Jesus said, "Let the little children come to Me, and do not hinder them, for the kingdom of God belongs to such as these"   Luke 18:16.

This can be done by printing the verse on the top of the paper, centered, in landscape mode (horizontally). Allow enough room for handprints underneath the verse.

3. Cut foam paper into the following sized rectangle. Each craft will require two pieces of foam paper 8 1/2" x 2" in size and two pieces 11" x 2" in size. These will be used to create a frame around the paper.

Assembling:

1. Glue the pre-printed verse page to the manila folder, by using a glue stick or putting glue on the corners of the back of the paper.

2. Paint the bottom of each child's hand with water-color paint and carefully put his or her handprints on the verse paper below the writing. Do one hand at a time, followed by clean up with baby wipes or soap and water. This may need to be done one child at a time.

3. Select two short rectangles and two long rectangle for the frame.

4. Glue the two short rectangles to the verse page. This will create the top and bottom of the frame. Then glue the two longer rectangles to create the sides.

5. Decorate the frame by randomly applying glue dots around the frame and then selecting various craft items to place on the glue dots.

6. Trim any excess folder showing outside the frame.

Other Ideas:

1. Use glitter glue to decorate the frame.

2. Use small shirt boxes or other cardboard like materials instead of the manila folders.

3. Create a pre-cut frame from large gift boxes or from post paper and then paint the frame and decorate it.

4. Trace the child's hand on the paper if painting is too messy or not an option.

The Last Supper
Mark 14:12-25

On the night before He was going to die, Jesus celebrated Passover, the Feast of Unleavened Bread, with His disciples. This feast recalls the time when God called his chosen people out of their bondage of slavery in Egypt to the promised land. Moses told the people to sacrifice a lamb and put some lamb's blood on the doorposts. That night the angel of death came and passed over the houses of those families where the blood of the lamb was on the doorpost. The first born sons of Pharaoh and of all the people who didn't sacrifice the Passover Lamb died.

Jesus knew that as the Passover Lamb He would save people from eternal suffering apart from God. Jesus told the disciples that one of them would betray Him. Jesus knew that Judas would betray Him with a kiss. It would be better never to have been born than to betray the Son of God.

As they were eating the Passover Meal, Jesus took bread, blessed and broke it, and gave it to them, saying "Take and eat, this is My Body, which is given for you. Do this in remembrance of Me." And He took a cup, and when He had given thanks He gave it to them and said to them "This is My blood of the covenant, which is poured out for many. Truly, I say to you, I shall not drink again from the fruit of the vine until that day when I drink it new in the kingdom of God" (cf. Mark 14:22-25).

The disciples sang a hymn and then went out to the Mount of Olives. Jesus told them that they would all run away from Him. But Peter said that he would never betray Jesus. Jesus told Peter that this very night, before the cock crowed, Peter would deny Jesus three times.

Jesus went to the Garden of Gethsemane to pray. He asked the disciples to pray with Him. But the disciples were very sleepy. They had eaten a big meal and drunk some wine and they could not keep their eyes open. So, Jesus prayed alone to His Father in heaven. Jesus was sad that His apostles could not stay awake and pray with Him.

Judas came to the Garden of Gethsemane and betrayed Jesus with a kiss. Peter denied Jesus three times and the cock crowed, just as Jesus predicted. The soldiers took Jesus away.

Judas despaired and hung himself. Peter repented of his sin. Peter was so sorry that he had denied Jesus. He remembered what Jesus had told him. Peter knew Jesus is God and that Jesus knows all things. Jesus knew Peter would deny Him, but Jesus kept on loving Peter anyway.

Jesus loves you. He knows that sometimes you will sin, but He keeps on loving you anyway. It is important to go to Jesus and tell Him you are sorry when you sin. Catholics go to Jesus in the Sacrament of Reconciliation to confess their sins to the priest and receive forgiveness and the grace to start anew.

When you are older, you will make your First Confession. The Sacrament of Penance enables us to be free from sin. Every time you sin, you can go to Confession, receive God's mercy and start anew.

At the Last Supper Jesus instituted the Holy Eucharist. When you are older, you can receive Jesus in the Blessed Sacrament. You must be free from sin with a pure soul to receive Holy Communion worthily.

The Sacraments of Penance and Eucharist are treasures of the faith that give us grace. They are our food for the journey to sustain us until we get to the next world. We call Holy Communion the Bread of Heaven.

"Take and eat. This is my body which is given for you. Do this in remembrance of me."

The Last Supper

 # The Last Supper Craft

The children can make a colorful place mat with a picture of the Last Supper.

Materials:

construction paper, picture of the Last Supper, crayons, glue or glue sticks, clear contact paper, scissors

Preparation:

1. Cut pieces of clear shelf paper 18" x 12" to cover the construction paper.

2. Trace and cut small Chalice shapes and Eucharist shapes from construction paper (two each per craft).

3. Remove the illustration, "The Last Supper," from the book.

Assembling:

1. Color "The Last Supper" illustration with crayons.

2. Cut out the silhouette of the Last Supper.

3. Glue the silhouette to the center of a piece of construction paper.

4. Glue the pre-cut Chalice and Eucharist shapes to the corners of the paper, or draw them if desired. Add the title "The Last Supper" along the center top and, if there is room, add the words "Do this in remembrance of Me" along the bottom.

5. Peel the back off the clear contact paper and place the craft, face down, along the side of the shelf paper (long side of paper by the 12" side of contact paper). Fold the shelf paper around the craft completely and cut off any extra. The Last Supper place mat is now complete.

Other Ideas:

1. Use adhesive plastic wrap, like clinging saran wrap, instead of contact paper. Tape down the edges.

2. Use foam paper instead of construction paper for a thicker place mat.

The Crucifixion
John 19:14-30

People were mad at Jesus because He called God His Father. How could a man be God? They thought Jesus was blaspheming the name of God! Jesus was arrested and taken to Pontius Pilate. Pilate asked Jesus, "Are you the King of the Jews?" Jesus said "My kingship is not of this world . . . I was born and have come into the world to bear witness to the truth." Pilate said to Jesus "What is truth?" (John 18:33, 35-37).

Pilate had Jesus scourged and put a crown of thorns on His head and clothed Him in a purple robe. People beat Jesus with whips, spit at Him, and put thorns on His head.

Jesus was bleeding. Then they made Jesus carry a cross and walk to Golgotha. Jesus fell three times walking under the weight of the cross. Simon of Cyrene helped Jesus carry His cross part of the way. When Jesus arrived at Golgotha, soldiers stripped off his cloak and nailed His hands and feet to the cross. The soldiers took Jesus' clothes and they cast lots for his tunic, which was woven without a seam.

Jesus was crucified between two criminals, even though Jesus had done nothing wrong. One criminal taunted Jesus and told Him to save Himself and them. But the other criminal, Dismas, said, "Don't you fear God? We deserve this punishment for our bad deeds, but Jesus has done nothing wrong." Then Dismas said, "Jesus, remember me when You come into Your kingdom." Jesus promised Dismas, "Truly, I say to you, today you will be with me in Paradise" (Luke 23:39-43).

Three Marys: Mary, the mother of Jesus, her sister, Mary the wife of Clopas, and Mary Magdalene were all standing by the cross crying. When Jesus saw His mother and the apostle John at the foot of the cross, He said to His mother, "Woman, behold your son!" Then to John, He said, "Behold, your mother!" Then John took the Blessed Mother into his own home and loved her and cared for her.

Jesus knew that He had done everything to fulfill the scriptures and said "I thirst." Some soldiers put sour, bitter vinegar on a sponge and held it to His mouth. Then Jesus said "It is finished"; and He bowed His head and gave up His Spirit. (John 19:28-30). Jesus died for your sins, and my sins, and the sins of the whole world.

When Jesus died on the cross, the thick curtain in the temple was ripped in two from top to bottom; the earth shook and the rocks split. Tombs opened and many of the saints, who had been dead, came out of their tombs and went into the holy city and appeared to many. The centurion who was with Jesus saw the earthquake, was filled with awe, and said, "Truly this was the Son of God!" (Matthew 27:51-54).

Then a rich man, Joseph of Arimathea, asked Pilate for the body of Jesus. Joseph took Jesus' body and wrapped it in a clean linen shroud and laid it in his own new tomb. Pilate's soldiers rolled a big stone over the opening of the tomb and soldiers guarded the tomb (Matthew 27:57-66).

We call this day Good Friday. It was a sad day for all of the people who love Jesus. Good Friday is the day when we recall our sins and how good Jesus is to die for those sins and take the punishment that we deserve. On Good Friday Catholics don't eat meat as a form of penance. We give up some things in Lent to show God that we are sorry for our sins. We thank Jesus for dying for our sins and the sins of the world.

The Crucifixion

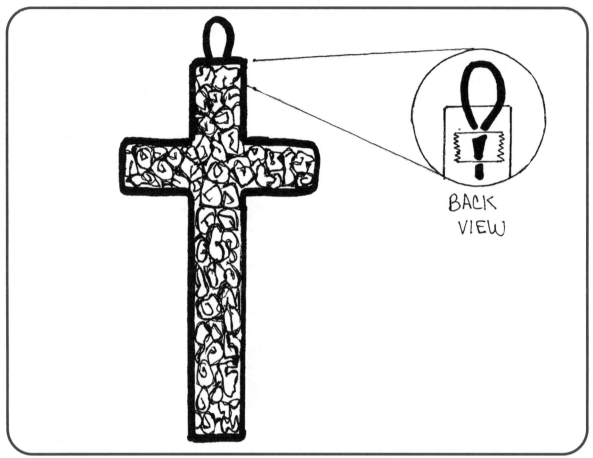

BACK VIEW

This craft will make a large, colorful cross that can be hung on the wall.

Materials:

heavy-stock brown construction paper, yarn, glue, scissors, tape, various colors of tissue paper, pipe cleaners (optional)

Preparation:

1. Trace the shape of a large cross on each piece of construction paper.

2. Cut small 3" x 3" pieces of tissue paper of various colors. Each craft will require at least 30 of these pieces of tissue paper.

Assembling:

1. Cut the cross out of construction paper.

2. Put glue along the perimeter of the cross and attach yarn to it. This will give the appearance of the outline of the cross.

3. Crumple up each piece of tissue paper and glue it to the inside of the cross. Continue to do this with different colors until the cross is completely filled in to make a stained glass look.

4. Tape a small loop of yarn to the top back of the cross after it has dried well.

Other Ideas:

1. Use poster paper instead of construction paper for a sturdier cross. Cut the poster paper into smaller pieces (8 1/2" x 11") prior to tracing a cross on it.

2. Create a crucifix instead of a cross. Make Jesus from pipe cleaners or by cutting out a picture of Him with His arms extended outward and glue Him to the cross.

The Resurrection
John 20:1-30

How sad Mary and the apostles were on Good Friday. Jesus was dead. Jesus loved everybody. Jesus fed the people when they were hungry. He took five loaves and two fishes and fed thousands of people. He cured the lame and the blind and the deaf. Jesus showed mercy to sinners. Jesus was kind to people that nobody liked. Jesus was so good. How could Pilate have sent Jesus to the cross? How could the soldiers have beaten Him and crucified Him so mercilessly?

On Easter Sunday, Mary Magdalene and Mary the mother of James went to the tomb with some spices to anoint Jesus' dead body. On the way to the tomb the women asked one another "Who will roll away the stone from the entrance to the tomb for us?"

The earth quaked and an angel of the Lord came down from heaven, rolled back the stone and sat on it. When the women arrived at the grave, they found the stone rolled away and they entered the tomb. But, they did not find the dead body of Jesus. Only the burial clothes remained in the sepulcher, but Jesus was gone! Where was the body of Jesus?

Mary Magdalene started crying. Did someone steal the body of Jesus? A man was standing by the tomb. Mary said "Sir, if you have carried Jesus away, tell me where you have laid him." The man said to her "Mary." She turned and saw that it was Jesus who was speaking to her. She said "Rabboni" (which means Teacher). Jesus said to her, "Do not hold me for I have not yet ascended to the Father; but go to my brethren and say to them, I am ascending to my Father and your Father, to my God and your God" (John 20:13-18).

Mary was so happy! She ran to tell the disciples that Jesus was alive! Who would believe Mary Magdalene? Who could believe that Jesus was alive? Everyone had seen Jesus on the cross bleeding. They saw Jesus die.

Simon Peter and John raced to the tomb. John was faster than Peter and got there first. But John respected Peter and waited for him to enter the tomb first. Peter and John went into the tomb, but they did not find Jesus. What do you think they found? Only the burial clothes were left in the tomb.   The dead body of Jesus was not there. Do you know what happened?

Jesus rose from the dead. Jesus died for our sins and the sins of the whole world and He rose from the dead. Jesus had the power to raise Jairus' daughter from death.   Jesus brought His friend, Lazarus back to life. Now Jesus came to life after His own death to show us that He is God. Death has no power over Jesus. Jesus conquered sin and death once and for all. Jesus lives! Jesus lives forever and so will we.

On Easter Sunday, we shout the good news to everyone we see.

Jesus Lives!
    He is Risen.
        He is Risen Indeed!
            Alleluia!   Alleluia!

Just as Jesus rose from the dead, we believe that Jesus will bring us to new life after we die. Don't be afraid of death. After death, eternal life in heaven awaits all those who love God.

The Resurrection

The Resurrection Craft

The children can create an Easter decoration of Jesus' empty tomb.

Materials:

picture of the empty tomb, paper plate, yarn, crayons or markers, paper puncher, tape, scissors

Preparation:

1. Remove the illustration, "The Resurrection," from the book.

2. Cut one 18" piece of yarn per child.

3. Put tape around one end of the yarn to make a needle and tie a knot around the other end.

Assembling:

1. Color "The Resurrection" picture using crayons or markers.

2. Cut out the people and the rock from the illustration.

3. Cut the paper plate in half. Then cut a half circle out of the bottom of one of the plate halves (this will be the entrance to the tomb).

4. Hold the two halves of the plates together (inside to inside) and tape it temporarily together.

5. Punch holes 1" apart along the curved sides.

6. Lace the yarn through the holes around the curved sides. Cut and tape the extra yarn to the back of the plate.

7. Write **"HE IS RISEN"** on the inside plate behind the cut-out half circle (inside the tomb).

8. Glue the cut-out people and rock to the outside of the tomb. This will create a lovely Resurrection scene that can stand on a table as an Easter decoration.

Other Ideas:

1. Use a paper fastener to attach the rock to the tomb. By turning the rock back and forth it will appear as though it is covering and then uncovering the empty tomb.

2. Staple or glue the plate together to eliminate the lacing.

3. Draw a shroud instead of writing "He is Risen" in the empty tomb.

4. Glue a small white piece of material in the tomb to represent the shroud of Jesus.

Jesus Lives!
Luke 24:13-35

On Easter Sunday night, the disciples were waiting in the upper room with the doors shut tight because they were afraid. Jesus walked straight through the closed doors and stood before them. Jesus said "Peace be with you." Then He showed the apostles the nail holes in His hands and feet, where He had been nailed to the cross. The disciples were glad to see Jesus risen from the dead.

Jesus breathed on the apostles and said "Receive the Holy Spirit. If you forgive the sins of any, they are forgiven; if you retain the sins of any, they are retained" (John 20:22-23). In this way, Jesus gave the apostles the power to forgive sins. This power from the Holy Spirit passes on in the Sacrament of Holy Orders to priests today. We go to Confession, and tell the priest our sins and that we are sorry and will try not to sin anymore. We know that the priest has power from Jesus to forgive all of our sins. The prayer we say in Confession is the Act of Contrition.

Act of Contrition

Oh my God, I am heartily sorry for having offended You.

I detest all my sins

because they offend You, my God,

who are all good and deserving of all my love.

I firmly resolve, with the help of your grace,

to sin no more

and to avoid the near occasion of sin.

Amen.

Thomas was not with the disciples when Jesus came into the room. The apostles told Thomas, "We have seen the Lord." But Doubting Thomas would not believe them. He said "Unless I see in his hands the print of the nails, and place my finger in the mark of the nails, and place my hand in his side, I will not believe" (John 20:25).

Eight days later, Jesus walked through the closed doors once again and said "Peace be with you." Then He said to Doubting Thomas, "Put your finger here and see My hands; put out your hand, and place it in my side; do not be faithless, but believing."

You believe because you have seen. "Blessed are those who have not seen and yet believe" (John 20:27-29).

That same day, two disciples were walking to the village of Emmaus and talking about Jesus dying on the cross. While they were walking and talking, Jesus joined them. They did not recognize Jesus, because Jesus had a glorified body.

Soon Jesus started to explain to them from the Bible why the Son of God had to suffer and die for man's sins. When they stopped for the evening meal, He was at table with them. Jesus took the bread, blessed and broke it, and gave it to them. Then their eyes were opened, and they recognized Jesus in the breaking of the bread. Then He vanished from their sight. They said "Did not our hearts burn within us while He talked to us on the road . . .(and) opened to us the scriptures?" They found the eleven apostles and said, "The Lord has risen indeed!" (Luke 24:30-34).

Jesus stayed on earth for forty days after His death and Resurrection. He made breakfast for the disciples on the beach, cooking some fish for them. He gave the disciples great joy and many people saw Jesus walking and talking after He died and rose from the dead. Soon it was time for Jesus to go back up to heaven to be with God the Father. Before He ascended into heaven, Jesus said, "Go therefore and make disciples of all nations, baptizing them in the name of the Father and of the Son and of the Holy Spirit, teaching them to obey all that I commanded you; and lo, I am with you always, to the end of the age" (Matthew 28:19-20).

Jesus went up into heaven in a cloud while the disciples were watching Him. Two angels said "Jesus will come back in the same way as you have seen him go (into heaven)" (Acts 1:11,JB). We know that Jesus is with us and we await the day when Jesus will come again in glory with a trumpet blast. Until Jesus comes again in glory, we love Him and pray to Him and we are as good as we can be. Do you know how to tell someone the good news about Jesus? What would you say if someone asked you about Jesus?

Jesus is God. He came to earth as a baby. Jesus worked many miracles. He made the blind see and the deaf hear.

Jesus died on the cross for my sins and the sins of the world. And Jesus rose from the dead. Jesus lives!

I love You, Jesus!

I hope to see You one day in Heaven, Jesus, with God the Father and the Holy Spirit.

Jesus Lives!

Jesus Lives Craft

This craft will make a butterfly refrigerator magnet that reads "JESUS LIVES!"

Materials:

pipe cleaners, assorted colors of tissue paper, clothespins, glue, scissors, markers, magnets (stick-on)

Preparation:

1. Pre-cut 5" x 5" squares of tissue paper in assorted colors. Two squares are needed for each butterfly.

Assembling:

1. Fold a pre-cut square of tissue paper diagonally. Then accordion fold the triangle from center to the end point in equal folds.

2. Open up the square and refold one side to have the folds all going in the same direction.

3. Fold and crease the square in the middle.

4. Put two folded squares of tissue paper together and wrap a pipe cleaner, starting from the middle of the pipe cleaner, around the middle folds to make the butterfly wings. Leave a little extra pipe cleaner for the antennae.

5. Clip the end of the clothespin to the center of the butterfly wings.

6. Bend the ends of the pipe cleaners to look like antennae.

7. Write "JESUS LIVES!" on the clothespin. The butterfly is complete!

8. Peel and stick the magnet to the back of the butterfly, or glue a magnet on.

Other Ideas:

1. Make a butterfly mobile by assembling multiple butterflies and hanging them from a hanger.

2. Eliminate the magnet and use the butterfly as a finger puppet.

3. Decorate the butterflies with glitter or glue little eyes on the butterfly.